101
STEM JOKES

**ROCKETSHIPSQUID**

ISBN: 978-0-578-66003-5
Published by Rocketshipsquid
1700 7th Avenue, Suite 252
Seattle, WA 98101

## DEDICATION

I would like to dedicate this book to Mom, Dad, and Nana, for helping me and to my brother Djai, Uncle Daoud, and Grandpa David for encouraging my humor, and my entire family.

# CONTENTS

# ABOUT THIS JOKE BOOK

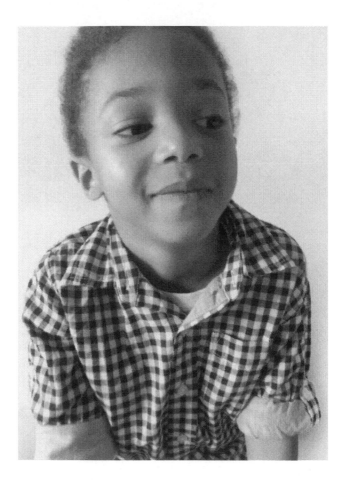

My name is Orion. I'm an award-winning, creative kid, author, and animator. As a kindergartner, I began writing funny stories in blank white books from the art store and sharing them with my class. My parents taught me how to turn the stories into animations. My dream was to become an author one day.

As a second grader, I enjoyed making my classmates laugh. Alison, my teacher, made a deal with me. If I promised to write down my jokes at home instead of telling them during class, she would provide a special time during the day where I would be able to share my jokes. I found this deal intriguing and much better than sitting in the "take-a-break chair," a place reserved for basically anyone who was not cooperating.

Three years later, I'm finally ready to share my *101 STEM Jokes* with you. My jokes were inspired by what I learned in school and outside of school as well as my interest in science, technology, engineering and math. I love messy science, the Hyperloop, outer space, and slimy sea creatures like the "sea bunny." I'm super excited about the possibility of a moon base or a future colony on Mars.

I asked my Nana, Treva Primus-Fitts, Science Educator, to approve the experiments in this book. Mom and I had fun researching fun facts together, and Dad, the techie, encouraged robot jokes.

Humor can be used to help new information stick and to make learning more fun. I hope that you'll turn your good ideas into jokes to share.

# Write your own STEM jokes here:

# SCIENCE

**Did you hear about the hagfish who went to the party?**

He had a good slime!

*FUN FACT:* A hagfish is an eel-like creature that produces slippery slime from its glands as a defense mechanism when threatened. This enables the hagfish to easily slip away. Groups of hagfish can leave hundreds of miles of slime trails at the bottom of the ocean. The hagfish slime is the strongest slime produced by an animal.

## MAKE YOUR OWN FAKE HAGFISH SLIME!

You will need:

1 half bottle (or 2.5 ounces) of clear craft glue

1 1/2 tbsp of contact lens solution

1/2 tsp baking soda

Mix the ingredients in a bowl until it forms slime.

Knead slime for about one minute until baking soda is no longer visible. Keep slime in an air safe container to store.

What kind of pants does DNA wear?

Jeans.

What kind of pants does fancy DNA wear?

Designer jeans.

Fabulous!

*FUN FACT:* Why are your eyes brown or blue? It's because of your genetics. Genes, not the blue jeans that you wear, are made up of DNA or deoxyribonucleic acid, which is the hereditary material in humans and almost all other organisms. The information in DNA is stored as a code made up of four chemical bases: adenine (A), guanine (G), cytosine (C), and thymine (T). Everything about you, including your eye color, is passed on to you through your parent's code. Nowadays genes can be created or modified by genetic engineering, resulting in what is sometimes referred to as "designer genes."

**What happens when a worm gets a new habitat?**

A houseworming.

**Why do so many worms come to New York?**

Because it's the big apple.

13

*FUN FACT:* Worms live where there is food, moisture, oxygen and a comfortable temperature. If they're not happy with their habitat, they'll squirm away.

There can be more than a million earthworms in one acre of land. Squirmy!

The largest earthworm ever found was living in South Africa, it measured 22 feet long!

**What did the mother universe give birth to?**

A sun.

**Where do astronauts play baseball?**

In the gravity field.

**What kind of dog loves science?**

A Labrador.

**What did the vinegar say to the baking soda?**

Don't overreact.

*FUN FACT:* The reaction between baking soda (sodium bicarbonate) and vinegar (dilute acetic acid) generates carbon dioxide gas. You can witness the chemical reaction with this simple activity:

**BAKING SODA EXPERIMENT:**

You will need:

1/4 cup baking soda

1/4 cup vinegar

Pour baking soda into the bottom of an empty container. Slowly pour the vinegar in. Watch how the two react and eventually bubble over!

**What particle is good at everything?**

A proton.

*FUN FACT:* Everything we know is made up of atoms: you, me, the trees, the ocean. Every single thing in the whole entire world is made of atoms! All atoms have protons. A proton is a subatomic particle found in the nucleus of every atom. The particle has a positive electrical charge, equal and opposite to that of the electron.

**What did the chair do at the doctor?**

He gave a stool sample.

*FUN FACT:* What would you do if your doctor asked you to hand over some poo? Get to work on that good old number two! Scientist can tell lots about your health by studying your stool in a lab. Once you hand over your feces, the laboratory staff may do a stool culture, which means they will smear your poo on a special plate, then they'll grow the bacteria present in your stool. This will help them to learn if any harmful bacteria are living in your poop.

**What do you get when you cross an element with a mouth?**

Tungsten.

*FUN FACT:* On the periodic table of elements, tungsten is atomic number 74. It has the highest melting point of all of the elements ever discovered, melting at 6192 Fahrenheit or 3422 Celsius.

**What's a good fruit to eat when you're dehydrated?**
H20-melon.

**What does a frog eat when it's hungry?**
A mealworm.

**What kind of fish do you ride?**
A seahorse.

**What kind of sea creature is a celebrity?**

A sea star.

**What kind of fish talks too much?**

A big mouth bass.

**What kind of fish is out of breath?**

A pufferfish.

*FUN FACT:* When threatened, a pufferfish will puff up to a shape that is more than double its size. While you may assume that it uses air to puff up, the fish fills its stomach with water to achieve the puffy effect. When big and round and sometimes covered in spikes, it's much more difficult for predators to snack on. Pretty clever!

**What's does a fish call his friend?**
A chum.

*FUN FACT:* Fisherman use chum as bait to attract bigger fish. Chum is fish food made up of chopped fish parts.

**What did the little brother fish say when he got pranked?**

"Good reef!"

*FUN FACT:* One-quarter of all ocean species depend on coral reefs for food and shelter. The largest coral reef is the Great Barrier Reef, which sits off the coast of Australia and stretches across 1,600 miles. It is so big that one can see it from space! Learn more about coral reefs and why they're in danger at Smithsonian Ocean: ocean.si.edu

**Where did the crab go to sleep?**

In the seabed.

What do you
get when you
cross shellfish
with a protein
shake?

Mussels.

What do you call a rude sea clam?

Selfish shellfish.

What did sea creatures use in the Civil
War?

Swordfish.

**How do shellfish say: "Sit still?"**

"Don't move a mussel!"

**What did the seabird say when he was out of breath?**

"I'm a puffin."

*FUN FACT:* One of the many differences between puffins and penguins is that puffins can fly, and penguins cannot. A puffin can fly pretty fast, up to 55 mph.

**What did the bird say to the thief?**

"Stop robin my nest."

**Did you hear the bird who groomed his feathers?**

He was clean as a whistle.

*FUN FACT:* Birds use their beaks or bills to groom in a process called preening. Most birds have a preen gland near the base of the tail which produces an oily secretion. The bird uses its beak to spread the oil over its feathers, legs, and feet. This helps to maintain feathers and, in some cases, provide waterproofing.

**Knock Knock**

Who's there?

**Owl says.**

Owl says who?

**That's correct!**

who?

**What's a screech-owl's favorite dessert?**

I scream.

*FUN FACT:* When an eastern screech-owl's feathers are ruffled, it will let out a loud, alarming, screech, mostly when it's defending its nest. It will also clack its beak together as a sign of annoyance.

**What does a bird take when it's sick?**

A pill bug.

**What kind of rash do baby chickens get?**

Eggzema.

**What happened to the poor garden slug?**

It was a-salt-ted.

**What do spiders put on toast?**

Butterflies.

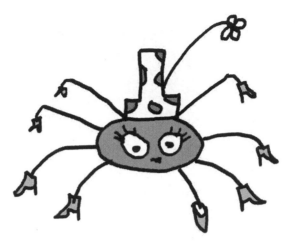

*FUN FACT:* A spider webs' sticky, flexible, super strong, fibers can stretch to capacity and then bounce right back into place without losing its original tension. And pound for pound, they're stronger than steel. That's why engineers are studying spider webs with hopes to re-create the material for applications in science, engineering, medicine, and maybe even fashion.

**What did the snake say when he missed out on dinner?**

"Rats!"

**What's an ant's favorite cake?**

Crumb cake.

**What did the leaf say to the pest?**

"Leaf me alone!'

**What's a honey bee's favorite activity?**

A spelling bee.

**What did the worker bee say at show and tell?**

"Beehold!"

**FUN FACT:** Scientists recently discovered that bees are very smart. Not only can they count, they have shown that they may understand the concept of zero, or nothing. The only other animals besides humans to show that they may understand zero are primates and an African grey parrot named Alex. Check it out at Smithsonian Magazine:

https://www.smithsonianmag.com/science-nature/bees-may-understand-zero-concept-took-humans-millennia-grasp-180969282/

**What do you get when you cross an intellectual with a worm?**

A bookworm.

**What happened to the eardrum at a loud concert?**

It got irritated.

**What do you call it when an ear goes to bed?**

Sound asleep.

**What instrument does an ear play?**

The eardrum.

**FUN FACT:**

The eardrum is a
membrane that
separates the
inner and outer
ear and vibrates
when sound
waves hit it.

When your outer

ear funnels sound waves into the ear canal,

they travel and hit the eardrum. In the inner

ear, the vibrations are converted into nerve

impulses that travel to the brain along the

auditory nerve. The brain interprets these

signals as sound.

**What did the funny bone say when the spine came to visit?**

"You're back again!"

**Which medical instrument makes your taste buds sad?**

A tongue depressor.

**What's a bat's favorite game?**

Baseball.

**Why were the hog's eyes red?**

Because of a lack of pigment.

*FUN FACT:* The pigment melanin is responsible for the color of your eyes. If you have more melanin in your iris, the colored part of your eyes, you'll have brown eyes. People with light colored eyes such as blue, grey, and green, have less melanin in the iris.

**What does a mouse have at a party?**

Cheesecake.

**What do you call a mouse with no sense of humor?**

Cheesy.

**Where do horses live?**

Neigh-borhoods.

**Who does a  Llama call when he has to move?**

An alpaca.

*FUN FACT:* Did you know that llamas and alpacas are both part of the camel family, Camelidae? You can tell llamas and alpacas apart by their size and features. Alpacas are smaller in size, ranging from about 121 to 143 pounds, they have small faces with short ears, while llamas have longer faces with banana-like ears. Llamas are also larger than alpacas and can weigh around 250 pounds. Don't get them confused or you may start some llama drama!

## What do sugar snap peas do when they're frightened?

Pea their pants!

**Which microbes like to party?**

The fungi.

*FUN FACT:* A microbe, or "microscopic organism," is a living thing that is too small to be seen with the naked eye. We have massive numbers of microbes living on and inside of our bodies, about 100 trillion of them!

**Why was the germ a big star?**

He went viral.

## What mountain do you climb at rush hour?

Mount Rushmore.

*FUN FACT:* Mount Rushmore was originally known to the Native American Lakota Sioux as "The Six Grandfathers" or "Cougar Mountain." It was formed when sediments at the bottom of a shallow sea began to rise during the Precambrian period, about 1.6 billion years ago. The huge mass of molten rock rose from deep within the earth's crust. As this mass cooled underground, it formed the granite which is now the core of the Black Hills. During an expedition in 1885, the mountain was renamed after Charles E.

Rushmore, a prominent New York lawyer. U.S. president Calvin Coolidge had the granite face of the mountain carved with the faces of U.S. presidents George Washington, Thomas Jefferson, Theodore Roosevelt, and Abraham Lincoln to attract tourists to the Black Hills region of South Dakota.

**What do you call a daydreaming astronaut?** Spacey.

**What's one of the smelliest planet in the universe?**

Uranus.

**Uranus is gassy.**

*FUN FACT:* Uranus smells like farts. It's really true! A recent study by University of Oxford, found that the seventh planet from the sun's upper atmosphere is made of hydrogen sulfide, which is the same compound that makes farts and rotten eggs smell yucky.

# TECHNOLOGY

## How does a robot eat pizza?

He takes megabytes.

## Why did the mobile phone go to the dentist?

To fix its Bluetooth.

*FUN FACT:* Bluetooth is named after a medieval Viking ruler named King Harald Gormsson. Reportedly, the King's nickname was Bluetooth or blátǫnn in Old Norse or Blåtand in Danish. King Bluetooth may actually have gotten his name from his old, rotten, blueish tooth. He was famous for uniting Denmark in the way that a group of companies: Intel, Ericsson, Nokia, and IBM, wished to unite in 1996. They hoped to create a single wireless standard to connect mobile phones, computers, and other electronic devices. The developers, fond of history, found the perfect namesake.

**Why did the horse eat the computer?**
Because it was an Apple.

*FUN FACT*: Steve Jobs and Steve Wozniak created Apple Computer on April 1, 1976, in Cupertino California. The name Apple was inspired by you guessed it, the fruit by the same name.

**What do baby computers sit on?**
Laptops.

**Did you hear about the robot who didn't wash his hands?**

He caught a computer virus.

**What did the coder say to the computer virus?**

"Stop bugging me!'

*FUN FACT:* The computer virus was designed by programmers to operate much like the organic version. *Achoo!*

Much like the flu, a computer virus is designed to spread from host to host and it even has the ability to replicate itself. Just as yucky, crummy, organic viruses can't reproduce without a host cell, computer viruses are unable to spread without a file, program, or document to attach to.

**How do platelets communicate?**

With cell phones.

*FUN FACT:* Platelets are a type of blood cell. If you fall down and scrape your knee, the platelets come along to help to stop the bleeding by clotting. Blood cells communicate with chemical signals, whereas cell (cellular) phones communicate through a network of radio signals.

**What's a head's favorite app?**

Facebook.

**What did the tablet say when he got thrown around?**

iPad enough!

*FUN FACT:* The first iPad was released by Apple computers on April 3, 2010. More than 300,000 were sold at launch, and by May 3, 2010, 1 million were sold. This created an entire generation of young iPad enthusiasts. The tablets made their way into homes, preschools, K-12, and higher educational institutions. As a result, developers began making a ton of educational apps.

**What do digital cameras cook with?**

Panoramas.

**What kind of program can swallow a goat?**

Python.

*FUN FACT:* When Guido van Rossum, Dutch programmer and creator of Python, began implementing his new computer language, he also happened to be reading the scripts from "Monty Python's Flying Circus," a BBC comedy series from the 1970s. He decided to call his computer language "Python" because the name was short, unique, and slightly mysterious.

# Why was the computer crying?

Because it wanted its motherboard.

**FUN FACT:** A computer really does need its motherboard! The motherboard consists of important circuitry that connects every part of a computer such as the CPU (Central Processing Unit), memory, hard-drive, and graphics chips.

**How did the computer get locked out?**

It couldn't find its keyboard.

**How do coffee drinking techies get places?**

They take the espresso lane.

**How does a spider do her shopping?**

She does a web search.

*FUN FACT:* The World Wide Web (WWW) was created by the U.S. Department of Defense/The Advanced Research Projects Agency (ARPA). ARPA developed the ARPANET in 1969, a network of mainframe computers at major universities. It was the first time that a set of computers were connected together for the purpose of sharing resources.

**How does a plant take a selfie?**

With photosynthesis.

**How did the giant get on the internet?**

With Wi-Fi-fo-fum.

*FUN FACT:* During World War 2, Hedy Lamarr, a glamorous Hollywood movie star and inventor, had the idea for a top-secret communications system called "frequency hopping," it would help to guide torpedos. Hedy's idea was to make both the transmitter and the receiver simultaneously jump from frequency to frequency so that someone trying to jam the torpedo signal wouldn't know where it was. This eventually led to what we know as Wi-Fi, wireless connectivity. This technology allows your laptop, PC, tablet or mobile phone to connect to the internet without pesky physical wires and cords.

**What do you call a unit with a short-term job?**
A gigabyte.

**A gigabyte is one billion bytes, that's more painful than a million!**

**FUN FACT:** The byte is a unit of digital information that consists of eight bits (binary digits). One megabyte is 1,000,000 bytes. One gigabyte equals 1,000,000,000 bytes. Gigabytes are used to measure the amount of information on any digital device. Pixels, texts, numbers, pictures, music, and video all take up bytes on a digital system.

# What's the main ingredient in robot trail mix?

Nuts and bolts.

# ENGINEERING

**How did the engineer solve the mouse problem?**

By building a catapult.

*FUN FACT:* Engineering is a field that combines science, technology, math, and design, to solve problems and innovate solutions. An engineer will start with a concept and move it through four stages: idea, design, build, and testing. Each invention may make our lives easier, such as Ben Franklin's light bulb and the Wright brothers' airplane. We're grateful to the engineers who invented:

**The Telephone** Alexander Graham Bell, a Scottish engineer in 1876

**The Train** Richard Trevithick, a British engineer in 1804

**The Computer** Charles Babbage, a British engineer in 1833-1871

**Automatic Elevator Safety Doors** Alexander Miles, an American engineer of African-American heritage in 1867

What inventions are you grateful for?

## Do you know what happens when you goof off in engineering class?

You get sent to the design principle.

*FUN FACT:* A design principle is not actually a person, it's a set of visual based guidelines that an engineer can follow to help solve creative problems such as principles of line, color, shape, and form to make a design visually appealing. An engineering team will repeat steps as many times as needed, testing out ideas and making improvements as they learn from failure and move closer to the perfect creative solution.

**How did the engineer design the playground?**

With a slide rule.

**Did you hear about the student who designed a tower out of marshmallows, chocolate, and graham crackers?**

The teacher was so impressed she asked for S'more ideas.

*FUN FACT:* You can think like an engineer by challenging your noggin to solve creative problems, try this simple STEM engineering experiment:

## ENGINEERING ACTIVITY:

You will need:

A pack of toothpicks and a bag of gummy bears

Can you build a tower using only toothpicks and gummy bears? How tall can you build your tower? Can you tweak your build to make it even taller and stronger? How much weight can it hold? Test the weight of your tower by placing various objects on top. If it falls, have fun trying to build it even stronger!

**Knock Knock**

Who's there?

**Lego**

Lego who?

**Lego my bricks, I'm building a spaceship!**

**Did you hear about the guy who invented the fan?**

Yeah, he was really cool!

*FUN FACT:* The hot guy who came up with the idea for the electrical fan was Schuyler Skaats Wheeler. He invented the first electrical fan in 1882. A few years later an inventor named Philip Diehl mounted a fan blade on a sewing machine motor and attached it to the ceiling, inventing the ceiling fan, which he patented in 1887.

**You know the guy who invented the toaster?**

His patent is worth a lot of bread!

*FUN FACT:* Charles P. Strite, an American inventor, received patent #1,394,450 on October 18, 1921, for the pop-up bread-toaster. Unhappy with the burnt toast they served at work in Stillwater, Minnesota, during World War I, he searched for a savvy solution.

**Did you hear about the woman who invented Kevlar?**

Her idea was bullet-proof.

*FUN FACT:* Stephanie Louise Kwolek was a Polish American chemist and inventor. She worked at DuPont for over 40 years. She invented the first of a family of synthetic fibers called poly-paraphenylene terephthalamide a.k.a. Kevlar. The ultra-strong, super useful fabric is best known for its use in bulletproof vests and knife-proof body armor. In 1995 Kwolek became the fourth woman to be added to the National Inventors Hall of Fame.

**You know about the guy who created the mechanical pencil?**

He sure was sharp!

*FUN FACT:* The Mechanical Pencil as we know and love it today was invented by Tokuji Hayakawa, the founder of Sharp. By developing a lead-thrusting device and inserting it into a metallic shaft, he revolutionized the way the world thought about pencils. At the time there was another mechanical pencil available, but it was made of celluloid which looked weird and wasn't a strong enough material to withstand everyday use. He eventually improved upon the construction and appearance of the existing device with the use of nickel.

**What did the axel say to the wheel?**

You're on a roll!

**FUN FACT:** Engineers often use simple machines to invent solutions to everyday problems. The six classic simple machines are:

1. lever

2. wheel and axle

3. pulley

4. inclined plane

5. wedge

6. screw

**What was the mouse looking for on the lever?**

A fulcrum.

**What did the elevator say to the pulley?**

"Give me a lift!"

*FUN FACT:* A fulcrum is the supporting point of a lever, which is a type of simple machine.

**What did the kid say to the broken seesaw?**

You're full-crummy!

**Did you hear about the robot hamster that won the science fair?**

It was a pet project.

**What do you get when you cross a snowman with dynamite?**

An a-bomb-inable snowman.

**What do you get when you give a maglev rail candy?**

A Hyperloop.

*FUN FACT:* Virgin's Hyperloop One, was founded on June 2014. It is a high-speed transportation concept that plans to use a linear electric motor to accelerate and decelerate an electromagnetically levitated pod through a low-pressure tube. The vehicle is expected to glide silently for miles at speeds up to 670 mph (1080 km/h) with no turbulence.

**Where does a train sleep?**

On a flatbed.

**What's a train's favorite drink?**

Ginger-rails.

*FUN FACT:* Granville Tailer Woods (April 23, 1856 – January 30, 1910) was an African-American engineer, who held more than 50 patents. Self-taught, he was the first American of African ancestry to be a mechanical and electrical engineer after the Civil War. He concentrated most of his work on trains and streetcars. One of his most famous inventions was the Multiplex Telegraph, a device that sent messages between train stations and moving trains. His invention created a safer and better public transportation system for the cities in the United States.

## Why did Leonardo da Vinci dream up the helicopter?

So he could roam Italy.

*FUN FACT*: In the 1940s, Igor Sikorsky, Russian engineer, released a working helicopter. It is amazing to note that Leonardo da Vinci, the famous Italian based artist and inventor, sketched a similar flying machine in the 15th century known as the airscrew. Da Vinci's airscrew concept measured more than 15 feet in diameter and was made of reed, linen, and wire.

# What is Nikola Tesla's Favorite Dance?

The Electric Slide.

**FUN FACT:** In the 1880s, Nikola Tesla, and his ex-boss and rival, Thomas Edison, waged "The War of The Currents" over whose electrical system would power the world. Would it be Tesla's alternating-current (AC) system, or Edison's rival direct-current (DC)

electric power? Tesla won as Edison's DC was super dangerous, with both citizens and animals accidentally getting electrocuted. AC is primarily used in the U.S. today. One exception is the electric railways in New York City's subway which exclusively employs DC

power between 110 and 1500 volts, to power its third rail system. If you happen to fall into the tracks near the dangerous third rail, you're toast!

# MATH

**What did the 2D shape say when it was paid a compliment?**

"You're flat-tering me!"

*FUN FACT:* Two-dimensional or 2D shapes are flat and only have two measurements: length and height. Three-dimensional or 3D shapes are not flat because they have a third measurement: length, height and width.

**What time do you learn geometry at school?**

Circle time.

**What did the clock say after his first slice of cake?**

"Seconds please!"

*FUN FACT:* Did you know that mechanical watches are more affected by gravity? When people want more accurate time, they rely on quartz watches. You got it! Quartz watches are run by quartz crystal.  A battery sends energy to a tiny piece of quartz crystal. The crystal vibrates independently of gravity, sending more accurate force to move the gears on the watch. Now you can be sure that you're on time, whether you're in an airplane or down in the ocean.

# How does a circle count?

By rounding.

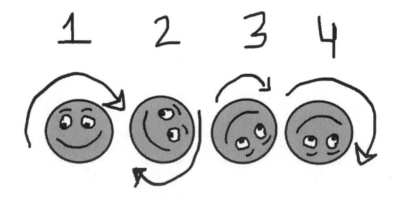

*FUN FACT:* Numbers can be rounded up or down to the nearest one, tens, or hundreds place on the number line. Rounding numbers is a breeze if you remember this simple rule: "if it's bigger than five, round up, if it's less than five, round down!"

**What do multiples eat dinner on?**

A times table.

*FUN FACT:* The multiples of the number 9 mirror themselves. Let's take a look:

9x1= 9, 9x2= 18, 9x3= 27, 9x4= 36, 9x5= 45

Now let's look at the mirror:

9x6= 54, 9x7= 63, 9x8= 72, 9x9= 81,

9x10=90.

**09, 18, 27, 36, 45 MIRROR: 54, 63, 72, 81, 90**

**Seven sure is an odd number!**

*FUN FACT:* Two odd numbers added together make an even number. Two even numbers added together make an even number. Only an even number added to an odd number can make an odd number.

Try it:

3+3= 6 **EVEN**

4+4= 8 **EVEN**

6+7= 13 **ODD!**

6+3= 9 **ODD!**

**How do accountants get home?**

They take taxis.

*FUN FACT:* People often refer to accountants as bean counters. An accountant is a professional tax expert who uses math to help people figure out exactly how much tax they owe. Tax is a percentage of money that the government takes from paychecks and businesses to use to fix things like roads, bridges, schools, hospitals and sports stadiums.  Counting with beans is actually a great way to learn math.

# BEAN COUNTING ACTIVITY

You will need:

A handful of

dried beans

Separate a group

of nine beans into

three groups of

three. You will see

that three groups

of three beans equals nine beans or 3x3=9. If

you take six beans away from your group of

nine beans, you will see that nine beans minus

six beans equals three beans! Or

9-6=3. You'd make a great accountant!

## How does a goldfish learn subtraction?

He goes to a school of fish.

## How do plants count?

By using square roots.

*FUN FACT:* The square of a number is the number multiplied by itself. For example, the square of one is one because 1x1=1, the square of two is four because 2x2=4, the square of three is nine because 3x3=9. The square of four is sixteen because 4x4=16. So, how do we find the square root of 16? The square root is the number that was used to create the square. The square root of sixteen is four because four squared or 4x4=16.

**What's a number's favorite sale?**

A 2-for-1 deal.

*FUN FACT:* There are many different types of fun triangles. In an acute triangle, the angles are less than 90°. A right angle has 90°. You can remember this by thinking that an acute triangle's angles are "cute" because they are smaller than 90°. How sweet!

**What do you call an adorable baby triangle?**

An acute triangle.

**Why did number 5 go to the gym?**

Because he wanted a six-pack.

## How did the ruler build his Kingdom?

Inch by inch!

*MEASURING ACTIVITY:*

Measuring things around the house is fun!

What you'll need:

A flat ruler

A washable marker

A piece of string that is 12" long

Wrap the string around your wrist, pinch the string where the ends meet. You can mark the point where the ends meet. Place the string next to a ruler and measure from the end of the string, to where you marked it with the marker. How many inches around is your wrist? Now have fun measuring everything!

# What's a fraction's favorite dessert?

A banana split!

**How do ducks pay for things?**

They use a down payment.

**What measurement of time can't even lift a pound?**

A week.

# Why do fours like to dance?

Because they love wearing two twos.

**How do you know that the number was telling the truth?**

Because he came from a good fact family.

*FUN FACT:* A fact family is a set of numbers or math facts that all use the same numbers. Pick your two favorite numbers, mine are seven and three. Now let's add addition and subtraction to make a fact family! Look, ten is a new member of the fact family!

**7+3=10, 3+7=10, 10-7=3 and 10-3=7**

**What does a pirate say when it's 20 degrees Fahrenheit?**

"Shiver me timbers!"

**What's a candle's favorite type of game?**

A matching game.

**Why was the teenage fraction happy for her 17th birthday?**

Because she was too over 16 (get it? 2/16).

**Did you hear about the bully who was learning his averages?**

He was mean.

*FUN FACT:* In math, the words mean and average have the same meaning. To find a mean or average, add up all of your numbers, then divide by the number of numbers. Here's an example:

In after-school,

**3** students are 5 years old (3x5=**15**),

**4** students are 6 years old (4x6=**24**) and

**1** student is 7 years old (1x7=**7**).

So that's **15**+**24**+**7**=46 divided by **8**, which is the total number of students. The result is an average or mean age of 5.7 years old per student.

**Why do digits need patience?**

To stand in a number line.

**What kind of desserts do numbers like?**

Pi.

## What is Pi squared?

Too much dessert!

*FUN FACT:* Pi is a famous number that equals approximately 3.14. Pi helps us measure how big circles are. If you had a pumpkin pie that was cut perfectly and you measured one slice from the middle to the outer edge (radius), the product of that number times itself (squared) times pi would tell you the area of your pie. $\mathbf{A = \pi\, r^2}$

## About the Author:

**Orion** was recently on New York City's WBLS radio show as a young filmmaker and

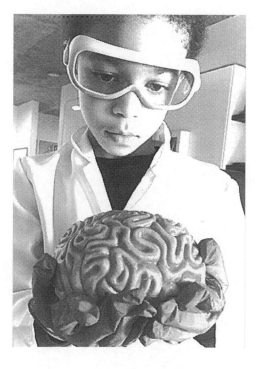

was honored by Jif peanut butter for his great storytelling in their "Imagine, Shared Stories" campaign. He received an award from Kids Who Bank, for his creative vision as a young entrepreneur. He is a winner in the University of Washington's 2020 Neuroscience for Kids Poetry Contest.

His journey in creating this collection of jokes was shared in a talk titled, "From Class Clown to Class Author" at The Seattle Times Ignite Education Lab. His animations were on display at Museum of Museums, Seattle, WA. Fill up on more funny stuff at:

**https://www.youtube.com/c/rocketshipsquid**

**instagram: @rocketshipsquid**

## Orion's Favorite STEM resources:

### Khan Academy:

https://www.khanacademy.org

### Splash Learn:

https://www.splashlearn.com

### BrainPop:

https://www.brainpop.com

### Code.org:

https://code.org

### National Geographic Kids:

https://kids.nationalgeographic.com

### Smithsonian:

https://www.si.edu/kids

Made in the USA
Middletown, DE
28 June 2020